No Lex 10-12

PEACHTREE CITY
PLAN TO STAY™

PEACHTREE CITY LIBRARY
201 Willowbend Road
Peachtree City, GA 30269-1623
Phone: 770-631-2520
Fax: 770-631-2522

Raven-Symone

Amie Jane Leavitt

P.O. Box 196
Hockessin, Delaware 19707
Visit us on the web: www.mitchelllane.com
Comments? email us: mitchelllane@mitchelllane.com

Mitchell Lane PUBLISHERS

Printing   3   4   5   6   7   8   9

A Robbie Reader
Contemporary Biography/Science Biography

Albert Pujols	Alex Rodriguez	Aly and AJ
Amanda Bynes	Ashley Tisdale	Brittany Murphy
Charles Schulz	Dakota Fanning	Dale Earnhardt Jr.
Donovan McNabb	Drake Bell & Josh Peck	Dr. Seuss
Dwayne "The Rock" Johnson	Dylan & Cole Sprouse	Eli Manning
Hilary Duff	Jamie Lynn Spears	Jesse McCartney
Johnny Gruelle	Jonas Brothers	Jordin Sparks
LeBron James	Mia Hamm	Miley Cyrus
Miranda Cosgrove	**Raven-Symone**	Shaquille O'Neal
The Story of Harley-Davidson	Syd Hoff	Tiki Barber
Tom Brady	Tony Hawk	

Library of Congress Cataloging-in-Publication Data
Leavitt, Amie Jane.
  Raven-Symone / by Amie Jane Leavitt.
     p. cm. — (A Robbie reader)
  Includes bibliographical references (p.) and index.
  ISBN-13: 978-1-58415-593-5 (library bound)
  1. Raven, 1985—Juvenile literature. 2. African American singers—Biography—
Juvenile literature. 3. Television actors and actresses—United States—Biography—
Juvenile literature. 4. African American actors—Biography—Juvenile—literature.
I. Title.
  ML3930.R28L43 2008
  791.4502'8092—dc22
  [B]   2007000787

ABOUT THE AUTHOR: Amie Jane Leavitt is an accomplished author and photographer. She graduated from Brigham Young University as an education major and has since then taught all subjects and grade levels in both private and public schools. She has written dozens of books for kids, has contributed to online and print media, and has worked as a consultant, writer, and editor for numerous educational publishing and assessment companies. Amie enjoys writing about people like Raven who work hard to achieve their dreams.

PHOTO CREDITS: Cover, p. 22—Fitzroy Barrett/Globe Photos; pp. 4, 6—Globe Photos; pp. 8, 11, 12—Judie Burstein/Globe Photos; p. 14—Evan Agostini/Getty Images; pp. 16, 18, 24—Frederick M. Brown/Getty Images; p. 20—John B. Zissel/Globe Photos; p. 26—Marsaili McGrath/Getty Images

ACKNOWLEDGMENTS: The following story has been thoroughly researched and to the best of our knowledge represents a true story. While every possible effort has been made to ensure accuracy, the publisher will not assume liability for damages caused by inaccuracies in the data, and makes no warranty on the accuracy of the information contained herein. This story has not been authorized or endorsed by Raven-Symone.

TABLE OF CONTENTS

Raven's first on-screen family: The Huxtables on *The Cosby Show.* Back row, from left to right: Theo (Malcolm-Jamal Warner), Dr. Cliff Huxtable (Bill Cosby), Clair Huxtable (Phylicia Rashad), Vanessa (Tempestt Bledsoe); center row: Elvin Tibideaux (Geoffrey Owens), Rudy (Keshia Knight Pulliam); front row: Sondra (Sabrina Le Beauf), Denise (Lisa Bonet), Lt. Martin Kendall (Joseph C. Phillips), and Olivia Kendall (Raven-Symone).

CHAPTER ONE

Olivia

One evening in 1988, Raven was watching *The Cosby Show* with her parents. Her favorite character on the show was Rudy Huxtable, the youngest child in the Huxtable family. Raven suddenly had an idea. "I can do what Rudy does," she said.

It wasn't unusual for Raven to say something like this. She was a smart child who liked to try new things. What was unusual was Raven's age. She wasn't quite three years old. Not many kids at this age would think they could do the job of someone on television. The great thing about Raven is that she didn't just *think* she could do it. She really *knew* she could, and she was willing to work hard to get what she wanted.

Raven works on the set of *The Cosby Show* with her onscreen grandfather, Bill Cosby. She loved working with the legendary comedian.

Just a short time later, Raven and her parents were in New York City. Raven tried out for a part on Bill Cosby's movie *Ghost Dad*. She didn't get the part because she was too young. Yet Bill Cosby liked what he saw. He thought Raven was a good **actress**, so he told her to memorize three pages of **script**. If she could remember her lines perfectly, he would give her a part on *The Cosby Show*.

Raven was very excited. She could not read yet, so she worked on her lines with her mother. Raven had a good memory and learned her part well.

Bill Cosby kept his word. He gave her the part of his granddaughter on the show. She would play the role of Olivia (oh-LIH-vee-uh) for three years until the show ended in 1992.

The Cosby Show was Raven's big break. It would lead to many great things for this bright child star.

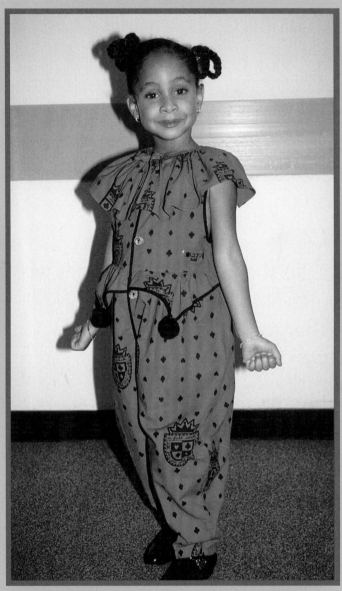

In 1990, before Raven turned five years old, she was already used to posing for photographers. She had been modeling for over three years.

Toddler Star

Raven-Symone (sih-MOHN) Christina Pearman was born on December 10, 1985. She is a Southern girl from Atlanta, Georgia. Her parents are Christopher and Lydia Pearman. She has one younger brother, named Blaize (BLAYZ).

Raven was a beautiful and happy baby. She had such a cute face and fun personality that she started modeling at 16 months old. Her picture was in magazine ads for popular products such as Ritz crackers, Jell-O pudding, and Cool Whip whipped topping.

In 1988, Raven got her big role on *The Cosby Show.* Her skills as an actress on this show helped her get many other parts later on.

After *The Cosby Show,* Raven continued to act for television. She played the part of Claudia (CLAW-dee-uh) on *The Fresh Prince of Bel-Air,* and the role of Nicole Lee on *Hangin' with Mr. Cooper.* Raven's first role on the big screen came in 1994. She played the girlfriend of Stymie (STY-mee) in *The Little Rascals.* Later she would play the doctor's daughter in *Dr. Doolittle* and *Dr. Doolittle 2.*

Not only is Raven a good actress, she is also a good singer. She says, "Though acting came first, I love to sing. At five, I told my dad I wanted to do my own album." That year, Raven became the youngest person ever to be signed with MCA Records. She recorded her first album, *Here's to New Dreams,* when she was eight years old. The CD features the single "That's What Little Girls Are Made Of." At the same age, she performed on Broadway in New York City. She sang with the Boys Choir of Harlem for their 25th Anniversary celebration.

Raven, who has always loved to cook, whips up a meal with her mother.

As Raven's acting and singing careers were blossoming, her parents wanted her to stay true to herself. They didn't want her to change who she was inside because she was famous. "Always stay sweet. Always be professional. And love what you're doing at all times," her mother would say.

In 1992, Raven helped out at a Ronald McDonald Fundraiser. Volunteering for charity has always been an important part of her life.

Just Like Other Kids

While growing up, Raven was not like most child stars. She lived in Hollywood only when she was working. The rest of the time, she lived in Atlanta. Most child stars have **tutors** (TOO-tors) and don't go to regular school.

Not Raven. Her parents wanted her to have a normal childhood, so she went to public school. "I went to homecoming, to football games, pep rallies," Raven says. "I don't feel like I've missed out on anything."

One of Raven's great loves is fashion. In this 2004 photo, she models her outfit for the cameras at *CosmoGIRL!* magazine's Fifth Annual "Born To Lead" Awards.

Raven's parents did not let her have an easy life just because she was famous. She did chores, kept her room clean, and did her homework.

Another way that Raven is different from other stars is her looks. Many stars are extremely thin. They go on diets all the time to look a certain way. Although she is physically fit, Raven isn't diet crazy. "My fans know I love my cheese grits and shrimp, and I'm not going to give that up to be a size two," she says.

Raven loves herself for who she is. She thinks that everyone is beautiful and shouldn't change just because of something they see on television. "I don't look glamorous all the time. I don't even worry about that type of stuff that much," Raven says. She doesn't like it when people try to be something that they are not. She always tries to stay real for herself and for her fans.

The cast of *That's So Raven*. From left to right: Corey
Baxter (Kyle Massey); Tonya Baxter (T'Keyah Crystal
Keymáh); Raven Baxter (Raven-Symone); Chelsea Daniels
(Anneliese van der Pol); and Eddie Thomas (Orlando
Brown). The show ran from 2002 until January 2007.

That's So Raven!

When Raven was 14, she started working for The Walt Disney Company. She was in a movie called *Zenon: Girl of the 21st Century.* She did such a good job in that movie that Disney asked her to do more work for them. She was the voice for the character Monique (moh-NEEK) in *Kim Possible.* She also starred in the Disney Channel movie *The Cheetah Girls.* In the movie, the Cheetah Girls is a singing group. The songs from the movie were sold as a CD. It sold over a million copies.

In 2003, Disney asked Raven to star in her own television show. It was called *That's So Raven.* Of course, Raven said yes. When

Raven's funny personality has helped her with her acting career. She has won many awards, including Nickelodeon Kids' Choice Awards for *That's So Raven.*

she did, she became the first African-American girl to have a television show named after her.

That's So Raven is about a teen named Raven Baxter who has special powers. She is **clairvoyant** (clayr-VOY-unt). This means that she can see into the future. Sometimes this gets Raven into trouble. Many times she does silly things that make her **audience** laugh. On the show, Raven's best friends are Chelsea and Eddie. They are played by Anneliese (AH-nah-LEE-zah) van der Pol and Orlando Brown. The three actors are good friends in real life too. "We'll help each other like a family does," Raven says.

That's So Raven has won many awards. Since 2004, it has won Young Artist Awards, NAACP Image Awards, and Nickelodeon Kids' Choice Awards. The show was also nominated for an Emmy in 2005.

Raven sang the theme song for her show, and she has continued to record solo albums. *Undeniable* was recorded in 1999, and *This Is My Time* was released in 2004. Her next album, *From Then Until . . .* was released in 2006.

The Cheetah Girls toured the U.S. without Raven in 2006. From left to right: Chanel (Adrienne Bailon), Dorinda (Sabrina Bryan), and Aqua (Kiely Williams).

Meanwhile, Cheetah Girl fans were very excited in 2006. That's when the group's second movie, *Cheetah Girls 2,* aired on the Disney Channel. Raven thinks the movie is good for young people. "The Cheetah Girls prove that not everybody has to look the same. Not everybody has to be skinny. Some people are comfortable with the way they are," she says.

The Cheetah Girls went on a tour around the United States in 2006, but Raven could not go because she had other jobs to do. One of them was to help out at the Stadium of Fire in Provo, Utah. This Fourth of July celebration was broadcast to the U.S. troops stationed in Iraq.

Raven has learned a lot about show business. At only 20 years old, she was co-producing *That's So Raven* as well as acting in it.

Looking Ahead

Raven loves singing and acting, but she likes to do other things too. She is a **humanitarian** (hyoo-MAH-nih-TAYR-ee-un), which means she likes to help other people. She has volunteered with Inner City Games and helps with the D.A.R.E. (Drug Abuse Resistance Education) program. She also helped with Colin Powell's Children First program and the National Safe Kids Campaign. She says she likes to help kids because "kids are the future and will one day run the country. So, we need to prepare children well so they can run the country with open minds and good hearts."

Raven is a classy and successful young woman. Besides acting, she also has many other interests, including producing television shows and movies and launching a clothing and cosmetics line.

In 2006, Raven presented the Children's Miracle Network with a check for $75,000. The money was raised by the That's So Raven "Eye on Fashion" benefit. Raven says that giving to charities "has always been a critical part of my life."

Raven has her own production company. It is called That's So Productions. Not many teens have done something like this. Raven was one of the **executive producers** of the third and fourth seasons of *That's So Raven*. She also helped produce *Cheetah Girls 2*. It is very challenging to be an actor in a show. To be both an actor and a producer takes a lot of talent.

Raven also loves to cook. She has many favorite recipes. One is for a dessert called crème brûlée (crem broo-LAY). Another is for a main dish called Cajun gumbo. Raven dreams of going to cooking school in Paris.

Along with cooking, Raven also likes to paint, hang out with her friends, and in the summertime ride jet skis. A fashion buff, she enjoys shopping for clothes, shoes, and makeup.

25

Raven is ready to make the leap from tween star to superstar. With well-laid plans, she's poised to grasp her goals.

If Raven could really see into the future like her television character does, what would she see? Hopefully, for the sake of her fans, there will be many more movies, television shows, and CDs. And maybe she'll even get to live her dream of going to cooking school. Yet it doesn't really matter what Raven decides to do with her future. If it's anything like her past, she will definitely be a success.

1985   Raven-Symone Christina Pearman is born in Atlanta, Georgia, on December 10.

1987   She lands her first modeling job.

1988   She tries out for *Ghost Dad* and doesn't get the part; instead she lands the part of Olivia on *The Cosby Show*.

1992   She plays Claudia on *The Fresh Prince of Bel-Air*.

1993   She releases *Here's to New Dreams* with MCA records.

1994   She plays Stymie's girlfriend on *The Little Rascals*.

1998   She plays Charisse on *Dr. Dolittle*.

1999   Her album *Undeniable* is released; she plays Nebula Wade on *Zenon: Girl of the 21st Century*

2001   She plays Charisse on *Dr. Dolittle 2*.

2003   She graduates from high school with honors. She plays Galleria Garibaldi on *The Cheetah Girls*; the album from the movie will sell over a million copies. She is the voice for Monique on *Kim Possible: A Stitch in Time*.

2004   She releases *This Is My Time*. She plays Nebula Wade on *Zenon 3* and Asana on *The Princess Diaries 2: Royal Engagement*, and she is the voice for Danielle in *Fat Albert*.

2005   She is the voice for Monique in *Kim Possible: So the Drama*.

2006   She plays the part of Brianna McCallister in *For One Night*, Galleria Garibaldi on *The Cheetah Girls 2*, and Marti on *Everyone's Hero*. The CD *The Cheetah Girls 2* is released.

2007   The last episode of *That's So Raven* airs. Raven is nominated for another Nickelodeon Kids' Choice Award for favorite television actress.

FILMOGRAPHY AND DISCOGRAPHY

Movies

2006	*Everyone's Hero*
	The Cheetah Girls 2 (TV)
	That's So Raven: Raven's Makeover Madness For One Night (TV)
2005	*Kim Possible: So the Drama* (TV)
2004	*Fat Albert*
	The Princess Diaries 2: Royal Engagement
	Zenon: Z3 (TV)
2003	*Kim Possible: A Sitch in Time* (TV)
	Kim Possible: The Secret Files
	The Cheetah Girls (TV)
2001	*Dr. Dolittle 2*
1999	*Zenon: Girl of the 21st Century*
1998	*Doctor Dolittle*
1994	*The Little Rascals*
1993	*Blindsided* (TV)

TV Shows

2003–2007	*That's So Raven* (also produced 18 episodes, 2006–07)
2002–2006	*Kim Possible* (15 episodes)
1993–1997	*Hangin' with Mr. Cooper* (34 episodes)
1993	*Queen* (TV miniseries)
1989–1992	*The Cosby Show* (33 episodes,)
1989	*A Different World* (1 episode)

Albums

2006	*From Then Until . . .*
	The Cheetah Girls 2 (with Adrienne Bailon, Sabrina Bryan, Kiely Williams)
2004	*This Is My Time*
2003	*The Cheetah Girls* (with Adrienne Bailon, Sabrina Bryan, Kiely Williams)
1999	*With a Child's Heart*
	Undeniable
1993	*Here's to New Dreams*

FIND OUT MORE

Articles

Bryson, Jodi. "Raven Is So Like That!" *Girls' Life*. October/ November 2004, pp. 48–51.

Feder-Feitel, Lisa. "Watch Raven Soar!" *Scholastic Scope*. February 23, 2004. p. 20.

Herr, Laurie. "A Big Little Star," *Winner*. March 1998, pp. 10–12.

Laufer-Krebs, Bonnie. "She's So Raven." *Kids Tribute*. Spring 2004, p. 21.

"Raven-Symone." *Scholastic Action*. November 3, 2003, p. 15.

Smith, Steph. "The Creative Spirit." *Scholastic News —Senior Edition*. May 9, 2003. p. 4–5.

"Spotlight" *Time for Kids*. September 17, 2004, p. 8.

Williams, Tia. "Shop Talk." *Teen People*. September 2003, p. 122.

On the Internet

The Official Raven Website
http://www.ravenlive.com

Raven's Music Site
http://hollywoodrecords.go.com/raven-symone/

Cheetah Girls
http://disney.go.com/disneyrecords/Song-Albums/ cheetahgirlsmusic/

Byrne, Bridget. "Raven-Symone, Cheetah Girls Go to Spain." *Bradenton Herald.* August 25, 2006.

"The Cosby Show." *People.* June 26, 2000, p. 68.

Gillespie, Fern. "Raven-Symone Plays Dr. Dolittle's Daughter." *New York Amsterdam News.* July 9, 1998, p. 21.

Goodman, Brenda. "That's So Refreshing." *Atlanta.* February 2006, p. 22–23.

"It's My Life: Raven Symone." PBSKids.org. http://pbskids.org/ itsmylife/celebs/interviews/raven.html

Keets Wright, Heather. "Raven Wins Raves." *Essence.* October 2003, pp. 148–149.

Keveney, Bill. "A Grown-up 'Cosby' Kid Returns to TV in Own Show." *USA Today.* July 11, 2002.

" 'Raven' Scent Meant for Tween Sensibilities." *Multichannel News.* October 3, 2005, p. 14.

Miller, Gerri. "Cheetah Girls 2." *Scholastic News Online. Scholastic News.com.* http://content.scholastic.com/browse/ article.jsp?id=7301

"Raven-Symone." *People.* April 17, 2006, p. 120.

"Raven-Symone (Music)." *People.* October 18, 2004.

"Raven-Symone: Sassy at 17." *TVGuide.com.* October 24, 2003. http://www.tvguide.com/News-Views/Interviews-Features/ Article/default.aspx?posting=%7BE4938E04-B207-43BA-ACA9-CF5B2A398CB1%7D

Samuels, Allison. "Why Not Raven?" *Newsweek.* August 1, 2005, pp. 50–51.

Smith, Scott S. "Three Questions." *Atlanta.* May 2000, p. 22.

Spector, Josh. "Raven Flexes Tween Power as Dis 'Girl.' " *Hollywood Reporter–International Edition.* July 22, 2003, p. 1.

"That's So Raven 'Eye on Fashion' Benefit Raises $75,000 for Children's Miracle Network," *Business Wire,* September 26, 2006.

actress (AK-tres)—a woman who performs in a play, television show, or movie.

audience (AW-dee-enss)—people who watch a play or show

clairvoyant (clayr-VOY-unt)—someone who can see into the future.

comedian (kuh-MEE-dee-uns)—a person who tells jokes and makes other people laugh.

executive producer (ek-SEH-kyoo-tiv proh-DOO-sur)—someone who supervises a show or movie.

humanitarian (hyoo-mah-nih-TAYR-ee-un)—a person who is concerned with human welfare.

script (skript)—the written text of a play, television show, or movie.

tutor (TOO-tor)—a person who helps to teach someone on a one-on-one basis.

INDEX